617

GW00771179

Frontiers of Surgery

Ann Fullick

www.heinemann.co.uk/library
Visit our website to find out more information about **Heinemann Library** books.

To order:
☎ Phone 44 (0) 1865 888066
📄 Send a fax to 44 (0) 1865 314091
💻 Visit the Heinemann Bookshop at www.heinemann.co.uk/library to browse our catalogue and order online.

First published in Great Britain by Heinemann Library, Halley Court, Jordan Hill, Oxford OX2 8EJ, part of Harcourt Education. Heinemann is a registered trademark of Harcourt Education Ltd.

Editorial: Lucy Thunder and Harriet Milles
Design: Joanna Malivoire and Celia Jones
Illustrations: Jeff Edwards
Picture Research: Melissa Allison and Liz Savery
Production: Camilla Smith

The paper used to print this book comes from sustainable resources.

Originated by Repro Multi Warna
Printed and bound in Hong Kong, China by South China Printing

ISBN 0 431 14905 4
09 08 07 06 05
10 9 8 7 6 5 4 3 2 1

British Library Cataloguing in Publication Data
Fullick, Ann,
Frontiers of surgery. – (Science at the Edge)
617
A full catalogue record for this book is available from the British Library.

Acknowledgements
The Publishers would like to thank the following for permission to reproduce photographs: Ann Fullick p**52**; Camera Press (CTK Photo/Maria Zamayova) p**16**; Christopher Sprod p**32**; Corbis (Paul Barton) p**57**, (RF) p**41**; Corbis Sygma (Collier Photos) p**55**; Dr Jeremy Southgate (Royal Bournemouth Hospital) pp**5**, **34**; Harcourt Education Ltd (Tinstar Design) p**27**; Mary Evans Picture Library p**8**; Medical Device Management Ltd p**21**; Photo Researchers Inc (Michael Donne) p**11**; Professor Brian Davies p**47**; Science Photo Library pp**7**, **10**, (Alexander Tsiaras) p**39**, (Alfred Pasieka) p**36**, (BSIP) p**49**, (CNRI) p**37**, (Custom Medical Stock Photo/Kevin Beebe) p**30**,(David Mack) p**54**, (Dr Gary Gaugler) p**50**, (Francoise Sauze) p**24**, (MIT AI Lab/Surgical Planning Lab/Brigham & Women's Hospital) p**12**, (National Cancer Institute) p**15**, (Nicolas Edwige) p**6**, (Peter Menzel) p**45**, (Tracy Dominey) p**4**, (Tek Image) pp**22**, **29**; The Image Bank p**43**; Trip/Archive p**56**; Wellcome Trust pp**19**, **35**.

Cover photograph of robotic surgery reproduced with permission of Science Photo Library (Peter Menzel).

The Publishers would like to thank Mr Jeremy Southgate, consultant orthopaedic surgeon, for his assistance in the preparation of this book.

Every effort has been made to contact copyright holders of any material reproduced in this book. Any omissions will be rectified in subsequent printings if notice is given to the Publishers.

Disclaimer

Contents

Any words appearing in the text in bold,
like this, are explained in the Glossary.

The miracle of surgery

Surgery – cutting open the human body to cure disease or mend things that are going wrong – is partly science, and partly an art. The skills of the surgeon, combined with advances in technology, are now making it possible to carry out operations that, only a few years ago, would have seemed impossible.

The human body is amazing, with many different organs and tissues working together to keep us alive and healthy. But when things go wrong we are in trouble. We may be in pain, or unable to do everything we want to, or our lives may be threatened. This is when surgery can come into its own – for conditions ranging from eye defects to cancer, the surgeon can offer hope of life-enhancing help.

Just imagine the skill required to separate twins joined together from birth, to replace entire organs or to operate on a baby before it has even left the womb. Advances in surgical techniques are happening thick and fast, making surgery that would not have been imagined a few years ago not only possible, but routine.

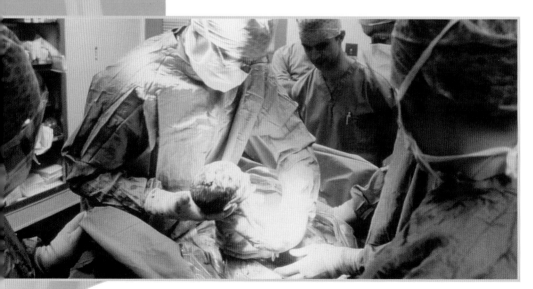

The Caesarean section to deliver a baby is a short but amazing operation, one of the oldest recorded types of surgery. However, increasingly Caesareans are carried out for the convenience of the doctors or the mother, rather than because the baby is in difficulty – and we need to ask if surgery should be used in this way.

Everyday surgery

Whilst exciting, cutting-edge, new surgery makes the headlines, most of the surgery that goes on in hospitals all over the world is less groundbreaking, but just as necessary to the people who need it. The replacement of arthritic hips that cause dreadful pain and lack of mobility, the delivery of babies by **Caesarean section**, or the removal of tonsils may not be glamorous, but they are all life-enhancing, and can be life-saving too. New techniques to make these everyday procedures safer, faster and less traumatic are being developed all the time.

Surgery of any sort cannot take place without an enormous amount of back up. **X-rays** and scans make it possible for doctors to see inside our bodies before they ever cut into the flesh, while anaesthetists keep patients out of pain – and often asleep – for as long as surgery lasts.

As surgery pushes the boundaries, with ever more incredible procedures becoming possible, different issues raise their heads. The massive cost of some forms of surgery, and ethical questions about some of the techniques now attempted, mean that the question 'Can we do it?' is increasingly being followed by another, even more difficult one – 'Should we do it?'

*'**Orthopaedic** surgery involves dealing with problems of the musculoskeletal system, from the victims of road accidents to conditions such as arthritis. It is becoming increasingly specialized, with surgeons concentrating on particular areas of the body. I specialize in hand surgery and find the job immensely rewarding – although it's always a challenge working in a health system with finite resources!'*
Jeremy Southgate, a British orthopaedic surgeon

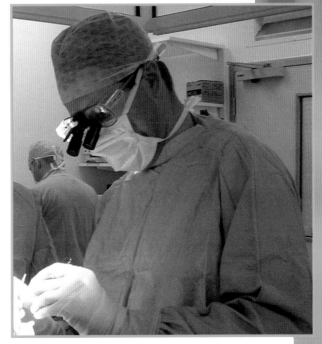

Jeremy Southgate at work.

The story of surgery

A modern operating theatre is clean, shining and sterile, with all the equipment needed to carry out the surgery and keep people safe. The doctors and nurses wear sterile clothing, scrub their skin and wear masks. Yet only 100 years ago, children had their tonsils removed on the kitchen table, using only a whiff of **ether** to keep them unconscious.

Stone Age surgery

The earliest beginnings of surgery were eight to twelve thousand years ago. The people who lived at this time suffered from many of the same illnesses that affect us today. The problem for them was that there was relatively little that could be done. However, there is astonishing evidence that our early ancestors carried out a simple form of surgery on people who were suffering from fractured skulls, epileptic fits and probably a number of mental health problems. They carried out a procedure called trepanning – making a hole in the skull to relieve pressure on the brain. This can be life-saving if it is carried out in situations where the brain is swelling due to injury, or if there is bleeding in the skull that is putting pressure on the brain. However, Stone Age surgery must have been pretty grim, with a fully conscious patient held down on

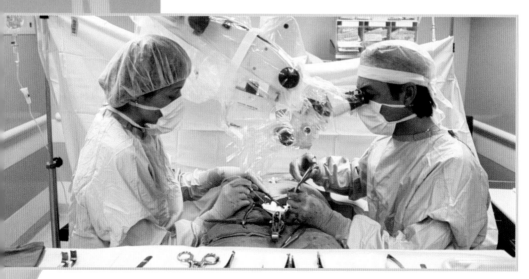

A modern operating theatre is well lit, well equipped and as free from the microorganisms which cause disease as possible, to avoid infection after surgery.

the ground while holes were forcibly made in his or her skull with sharpened rocks that were probably not very clean! Amazingly, we know it actually worked sometimes – or at least didn't kill the patient – because not only have ancient skulls have been found with the holes made by trepanning, some have been discovered with healed trepanning sites!

Barber-surgeons

For centuries surgery remained a brutal process, the part of medicine that no one really wanted to be a part of. In the Christian world, it was the Church, not doctors, who carried out any operations that were needed, until in 1163 the Pope decreed that monks and priests could no longer be involved in surgery. However, the barbers who cut the hair and beards of the monks and priests had no such scruples. They saw an opening in the market when the Church stopped offering surgery, and began to use their razors and knives for lancing veins and boils and carrying out amputations where necessary! The barber-surgeons developed a fearsome reputation, and no wonder. Their only form of **anaesthetic** was alcohol, and people only submitted to surgery as a last resort. The great majority of people who had surgery died within days from shock, blood loss or infection, although enough must have survived for the practice to continue. The red and white pole outside traditional barber's shops represents white bandages stained with blood, showing that they were willing to do more than give you a shave!

A barber-surgeon in action. The whole process was barbaric by our standards, but was the only hope for people with infected wounds in the days before modern surgery and antibiotics.

The arrival of the three As

Eventually the medical profession realized that surgery had the potential to be an important tool in treating disease, and doctors began to take over from the barber shops. In 1745 the Company of Surgeons, which would in time become the Royal College of Surgeons, was founded. No barber-surgeons were allowed to be members!

William Morton was an unqualified dentist who used ether in his dental surgery and spent much of his life trying – and failing – to make money out of his discovery.

Anaesthetic

Three discoveries made the development of modern surgery possible. The first was **anaesthesia** – the ability to put people to sleep whilst doctors operated on them. In 1842, Dr Crawford Williamson Long, an American doctor, used ether for the first time as an anaesthetic during an operation. He didn't publish his results until 1848, so the credit for discovering the first anaesthetic usually goes to William Morton, a dentist who published his work with ether in 1846. There were great rivalries among the early workers in anaesthetics – Morton ended up bankrupt and deeply unhappy and died aged 48 of a brain haemorrhage. At Morton's funeral, his wife is reported to have said 'My husband's great gift, which he devoted to the service of mankind, proved a curse to himself and to his family'.

The use of anaesthetics was probably the single most important development in the history of surgery. For the patient, it meant no more terror and agony, no more being held down whilst your body was opened up in front of your eyes. For the surgeon, it meant delicacy and precise work became possible because the patient was no longer screaming in agony. Anaesthetics gave surgeons the luxury of a still patient and time to consider what to do.

Antiseptic
The second big development was the use of **antiseptics**. Even with the use of anaesthetics, nearly half of all surgical patients died, mostly from infected wounds. In 1867, Joseph Lister started to use phenol in surgery. He soaked bandages in this chemical and insisted that everything in his operating theatres was clean. These precautions killed bacteria and so cut down the risk of wounds becoming infected during surgery. The overall death rate among Lister's patients dropped rapidly.

Asepsis
The final big step that had to be made before surgery could really take off was for doctors to realize the need for **asepsis** – that it was better not to allow germs to infect a wound in the first place than to rely on antiseptics to kill them once they were in place. From around 1878 simple procedures like washing the operating theatre down with antiseptic, using face masks to prevent bacteria passing from the surgeon to the patient and washing hands before surgery became normal practice in all operating theatres. It seems unbelievable to us now, but doctors in the past often moved from one patient to another without washing their hands first!

With the threes As – anaesthetics, antiseptics and asepsis – in place, surgery was ready to take off. In the following chapters, we will be looking at innovations in many different types of surgery – although IVF, organ transplants and reconstructive surgery will only be mentioned briefly as you can find out all about them in other books in this series.

9

Finding the problem

Before surgery of any kind takes place, the surgeon needs to know exactly what is wrong with the patient. Less than forty years ago, many patients had to undergo an exploratory operation before they had their real treatment – an operation to find out what was wrong. If the problem was so bad that surgery couldn't help, or it turned out there wasn't really a problem at all, then this investigative surgery was unnecessary.

Listening carefully to the symptoms described by a patient is very important, and so is a physical examination. But doctors today have a variety of other ways in which they can find out what is wrong without operating on you. The simplest of these are blood tests. These can be used to show a range of problems, from a lack of iron in a patient's diet to very serious illnesses.

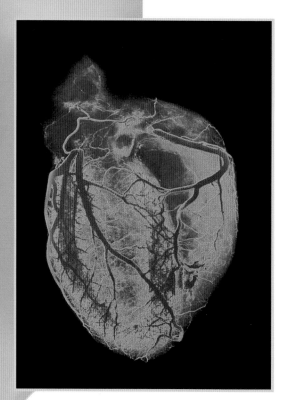

Angiograms enable surgeons to see if blood vessels are narrowed or blocked, and exactly how much damage has been done to the heart.

X-rays

X-rays pass through some body tissues but are absorbed by others. They also affect photographic film. An unexposed film is placed behind the part of the body that the surgeon wants to look at, and X-rays are focused on that body part. The film turns black where the X-rays get through the tissue, but stays white where the X-rays are absorbed. Bones show up particularly clearly. **Orthopaedic** surgeons who specialize in operating on the bones rely on X-rays to show them exactly what is wrong with a bone before they operate on it. X-rays taken after surgery can then confirm that things have been put right.

Soft tissues like the gut don't show up well on X-rays, but **radio-opaque** liquids, which are seen clearly on X-rays, can be used to make things clearer. For example, radio-opaque liquid can be injected into the blood vessels of the heart so that they show up clearly on the X-rays (called angiograms) that are taken.

CT scans

Surgeons no longer have to rely only on traditional two-dimensional X-rays to see inside our bodies. Developed in the 1970s, CT (Computerized Tomography) scanners allow doctors to see complete 'slices' through different areas of our bodies. The early scanners took four minutes just to build up an image of a single slice through the head. Scanners today can cover the whole body in a similar time! A CT scanner looks rather like a ring doughnut – the patient is laid on a platform that passes through the hole in the doughnut, while the X-ray tube and detectors move around the ring taking X-ray images from every angle. All of the information is fed into a computer, which builds up images of the individual slices of the body. The most sophisticated CT scanners can develop three-dimensional images of the inside of the body. The main disadvantage of CT scanners is that patients are exposed to a large dose of radiation, which can actually cause health problems.

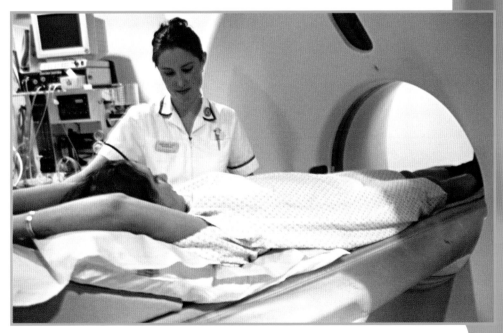

CT scans are painless for the patient, and the information they provide enables doctors to plan delicate surgery very precisely before they begin to operate.

Magnetic resonance imaging

For a surgeon, the more knowledge available about the condition of the patient, the better. X-rays and CT scans give excellent pictures of the inside of a body, but they both carry a slight risk of radiation damage. Magnetic resonance imaging (MRI) is still quite new – the first full-body MRI image was published in 1977 and took five hours to produce. It wasn't until the 1980s that whole body scanners were introduced in hospitals, but the impact of this new technology on medicine, and surgery in particular, has been incredible.

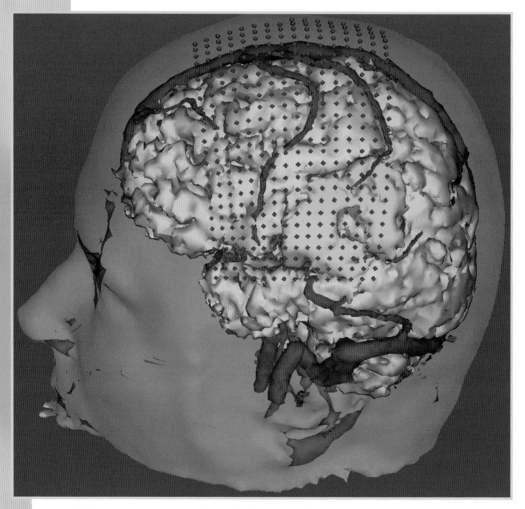

MRI scans are very popular with doctors and surgeons because the images are amazingly clear and detailed.

Swift and clear

High-quality images of the inside of the body can now be produced in seconds. This enables surgeons to see what is wrong with us, and operate to put it right, in a way that was impossible only a few years ago. They are also extremely safe because, unlike X-rays and CT scans, they do not expose the patient to radiation.

MRI uses a combination of radio waves and a strong **magnetic field** to form an image of the inside of the body. The scanner contains a powerful magnet, so everything metal has to be removed from patients before they go into the scanner room. The MRI scanner is a massive machine and the patient has to go right inside it to lie at the centre of the magnet, rather like the CT scanner. Because of the incredibly clear scans that MRI produces, the technology has made a huge impact in many areas of surgery – the images of real people now produced are as clear as the illustrations in an anatomy textbook.

Safe – but scary?

It is worth noting that this amazing new technology, which is such a tremendous help to surgeons in many areas, can be a rather daunting prospect for the patients who need to be scanned. One method of reassurance and support is given by providing the patient with a call button. If at any time they need become too anxious, they press the button and the procedure stops.

'I have had a number of different types of scan, but the MRI is the one I hope I don't have to have again! It is amazing to get such clear results without having an operation, and there is no pain at all, but it is quite an unnerving experience. I was strapped down onto the table and once you are eased into the tunnel it completely surrounds you and almost touches you. I was in the scanner for almost an hour and felt very isolated – I was really worried I was going to cough and hit my head!'

Dorothy Cane, a patient who has had an MRI scan

Ultrasound scans

Ultrasound scans use sound waves to form images of the organs of the body. Like CT scans and MRI, many of the significant advances in ultrasound scanning came in the 1970s and 80s. The first major use of ultrasound was to see inside the womb and monitor developing foetuses, taking care of them even before birth. Ultrasound has now spread far beyond the maternity unit and is used to examine almost every organ system of the body. It can be used to produce moving pictures, showing the supply of blood to an organ or **tumour**. What's more, the development of new computer software means that ultrasound can be used to produce three-dimensional images, which give surgeons a perfect model on which to plan their surgery. On top of this, ultrasound is relatively cheap compared to CT scans and MRI.

Nuclear medicine

Nuclear medicine is another important tool for the surgeon. For some years, surgeons have injected short-lived **radioisotopes** into patients, and then, using special cameras, have generated an image from the radiation produced. The radioactive compound used is carefully chosen so that it accumulates in the organ that the surgeon is interested in. The most recent cameras used can give three-dimensional images. The big advantage of this technology is that although it doesn't always give the clearest pictures of an organ, it is very good for allowing doctors to measure how well an organ is working – often much more important in diagnosis than exactly what it looks like.

Modern imaging

PET (positron emission tomography) imaging is the newest technique in nuclear medicine. PET technology is extremely complex, but it is already having an enormous impact on the treatment of cancer. PET imaging can detect small areas of active tumours which makes it possible to pick up the cancer much sooner than traditional methods allow. In turn, this means treatment can begin sooner and is more likely to be successful. PET imaging is also proving very useful in heart and brain surgery. There are also some very exciting developments using PET in studying the brain. It is now possible to image changes in brain activity when patients perform different tasks – PET lets doctors 'see' a patient thinking!

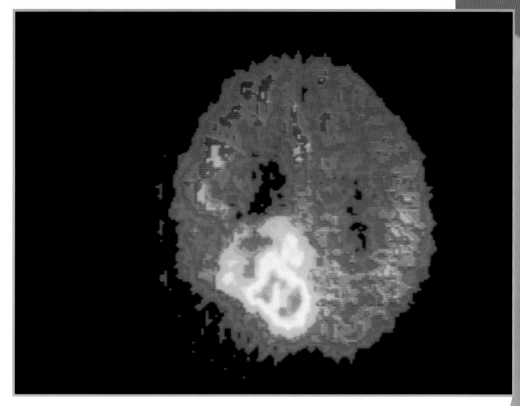

A PET image of the 'hot spot' of a tumour. This new technology allows doctors to detect many illnesses at a very early stage, giving the patient the best possible chance of recovery.

Imaging technology and surgery

Modern imaging technology has put an end to unnecessary operations, and dramatically improved the chances of successful surgery. Often, several types of scan will be carried out on the same patient, because each type of scan gives slightly different information. Although imaging, particularly PET, CT and MRI, is very expensive, it saves time and money in other ways by providing accurate diagnoses and making sure only necessary operations are carried out.

'...it would be difficult to overestimate the impact of the first ultrasound images. In the case of MRI, it would be an understatement to say that we were gobsmacked! ...When today's surgeon opens an abdomen, head or chest, they nearly always know exactly what they are going to find, because preoperative scanning has confirmed that disease is present, demonstrated its extent and often its exact nature...there are seldom any nasty surprises.'
Bob Bury, Consultant Radiologist and writer for
The Naked Scientist website and radio programme

Pushing the boundaries

The value – and limitations – of imaging technology are clearly seen when surgeons attempt to push the boundaries of what is possible. One of the clearest examples of this is in the separation of **conjoined twins**, formed when an early human embryo starts splitting to form identical twins, but does not split completely. It is a very rare condition, occurring in only one out of every 75–100, 000 live births and the overall survival rate of conjoined twins is low, at around 5–25%. Whether it is possible or not to separate a pair of conjoined twins depends largely on where and how they are joined together. This is an area of medicine where modern imaging techniques have made an enormous difference.

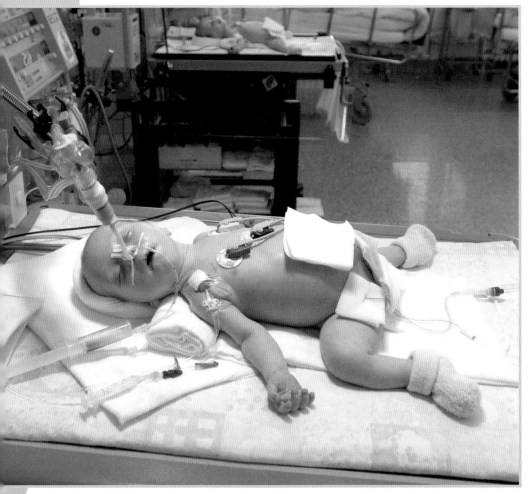

Slovakian twin girls, Andrea and Lucie, were born conjoined at the pelvis. Aged two months, they were successfully separated by surgeons from Bratislava University Pediatric Hospital.

Separating conjoined twins raises all sorts of questions. Often the life of one or both twins is at risk during surgery. Sometimes the only way to separate conjoined twins is for one of them to die, when a vital organ such as the heart is shared. In cases like these, who should make the decision for the surgery to go ahead?

The Banda boys

In 1997 Dr Ben Carson, an American brain surgeon, was asked his opinion about separating Joseph and Luka Banda, who were joined at the tops of their heads. An MRI scan showed that the twins' brains were not joined together, so surgeons decided that it should be possible to separate the pair. Using input from all the scans, the surgeons practised the operation in America using computer-generated images, before carrying it out for real in South Africa. The surgery was successful – the two boys were separated and are now living normal lives.

The courage of the Bijani twins

In 2003, the adult conjoined twins, Ladan and Laleh Bijani, decided to try for separation at the age of 29. Well educated and articulate, they were desperate to be independent of one another and to live their own lives. MRI, CT and ultrasound scans all showed that their brains were separate but that the blood supplies were intertwined. Several doctors refused to operate, but finally the Bijanis found a team in Singapore who were prepared to give them a chance.

However, once surgery got underway, the surgeons found that the girls had abnormally thick skulls, which had not been shown up by the imaging technology. Furthermore, the complexity of their shared blood supply had not shown up before surgery. After 52 hours on the operating table, massive bleeding which the surgeons simply could not stop claimed first Laden and then Laleh. The girls were finally separated, but only in death.

> 'Laden and Laleh were mature, intelligent women; they well understood the dangers and deserved their chance of independence, even at great risk...'
> John Harris, Professor of Bioethics at the University of Manchester

> 'First do no harm. Sometimes doctors are required not to do what patients ask for because their professional...assessment of the request is that it will cause harm, not good.'
> Dr Richard Nicholson, editor of the Bulletin of Medical Ethics

Anaesthetics

For surgery to be successful, it needs to cause the patient as little stress as possible. The ability to put patients into a chemical sleep so that they are unaware of everything that is going on has revolutionized surgery. **Anaesthetics**, and the anaesthetists who administer them, are a key factor in many of the advances that have taken place in surgery.

In the 1840s, three anaesthetics were discovered and came into use – **ether**, **nitrous oxide** (laughing gas) and **chloroform**. The impact of these **compounds** on surgery cannot be underestimated. However, they were not without their problems – ether is highly flammable, nitrous oxide only produces a very light level of **anaesthesia** and chloroform is toxic (poisonous) and can cause liver damage.

Of these three early anaesthetics, only nitrous oxide is still in use, mainly for pain relief during childbirth and after injuries rather than as a full anaesthetic. By the middle of the 20th century chemists were working to develop new, better compounds that could readily be inhaled, that produced deep sleep, yet were non-toxic and non-flammable.

The chemistry of anaesthetics

The development of new anaesthetics relied heavily on the work of chemists. They recognized two important features of chemical compounds which helped them in their search for better ways of sending people to sleep:

- Increasing the number of chlorine **atoms** in the anaesthetic compound increases the depth of anaesthesia given, but unfortunately also makes it more toxic.
- When carbon and fluorine are joined in a **molecule**, the bonds are very stable. Their presence in a compound tends to make it non-flammable, non-toxic and unreactive.

By adding both chlorine and fluorine atoms, chemists produced safe, non-toxic compounds that were also very effective anaesthetics.

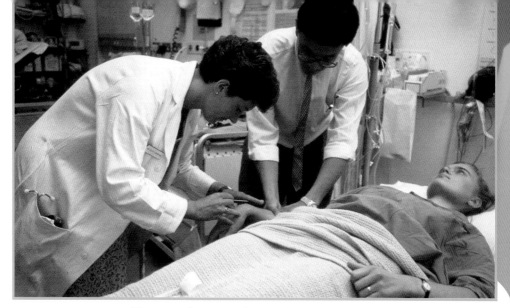

The anaesthetist works out the best type of anaesthetic and the amount needed for each individual patient and then gives them the drug just before surgery starts. It takes only a matter of seconds for the anaesthetic to take effect.

Safer sleep

In the 1970s, chemists produced the compound halothane, which gives deep yet safe anaesthesia. Soon afterwards, two similar compounds were developed – enflurane and isoflurane. These new anaesthetics have allowed surgery to progress so that operations are much safer for patients. An enormous variety of new surgical procedures has become possible. These range from operations being carried out through tiny openings made in the body wall, to massive transplant operations involving both patients and doctors in many hours in the operating theatre.

The fact that modern anaesthetics are not poisonous makes it possible for surgery to last more than 24 hours if necessary. They also make it possible for patients to have surgery and go home the same day, because the anaesthetic itself wears off fairly quickly and has relatively few side effects.

When the first effective anaesthetics were developed, the most important fact was that people were 'asleep' and unaware of any pain whilst the doctor operated. Some people died as a result of the anaesthetics used, but since many more people had once died from pain and shock when there were no effective anaesthetics, it was regarded as a price worth paying. Nowadays we do not tolerate such problems and scientists are constantly carrying out research to make anaesthetics even safer.

What happens in anaesthesia?

Successful surgery depends on successful anaesthesia. The anaesthetist has to make sure that the patient is unaware of anything going on around them and feels no pain. What is more, the muscles need to be relaxed so that the body's reflexes don't kick in as the surgeon cuts into the body. Controlling these reflexes is also the job of the anaesthetist. The use of muscle relaxants (chemicals to relax the muscles before surgery) was a major step forward, as it controlled the reflexes and meant less actual anaesthetic was needed.

Getting the right level

Not all surgery needs the same level of anaesthesia. A short operation on a finger does not require the same levels of anaesthetic as surgery to remove an entire organ and replace it with another, or to reconstruct a badly broken limb. The level of anaesthesia varies, and the anaesthetist has to judge what is needed for the surgery. What is more, the effect of the anaesthetic can build up, slowing the heart and the breathing more and more as time goes on.

During a long operation, the anaesthetist has to monitor the patient very carefully, checking their heart rate, breathing rate and blood pressure to make sure everything is normal.

Surgical anaesthesia

Controlling the level of consciousness is a very skilled job. Surgical anaesthesia ranges from light sleep to deep unconsciousness, depending on what the surgeon is going to do. The patient is unconscious, but just how unconscious varies depending on the amount of anaesthetic given. It ranges from relatively light anaesthesia, which suppresses the reflexes enough to stop the limbs or muscles moving as the skin is cut through, to quite deep anaesthesia, which prevents the abdominal muscles from tightening as the surgeon opens up the body.

In the deepest state of surgical anaesthesia, the patient undergoes respiratory paralysis. All the muscles are effectively paralysed and the patient has to be put on a ventilator to breathe for them. This level of anaesthesia is needed for major surgery such as heart transplants.

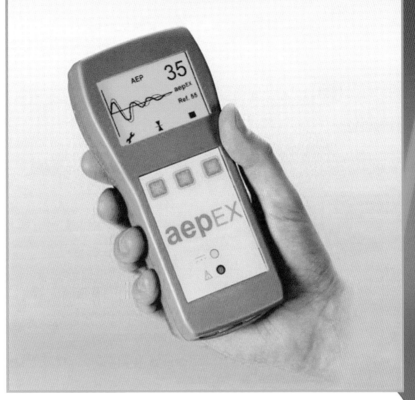

The aepEX system, which can be held in the hand or plugged into traditional anaesthetic systems, monitors consciousness levels by generating clicks in a patient's ear and then picking up the responses in the brain.

The latest technology

Traditionally, anaesthetists have monitored the state of their patients using large systems in the operating theatre that measure the levels of anaesthetic in the patients' blood as well as their vital signs. However, there have been some dramatic new developments in monitoring the levels of anaesthesia which may well move surgery forward even further. One of these new technologies is the aepEX depth of anaesthesia monitor, which has been developed over a ten-year period by Professor Gavin Kenny and his team at the Glasgow University Academic Department of Anaesthesia.

The aepEX system can be used to give an accurate guide to the patient's actual level of consciousness. This makes it possible for the anaesthetist to give the minimum amount of anaesthetic drug while keeping the patient at exactly the level of anaesthesia needed by the surgeon. This should make all surgery, but particularly long operations, very much safer, which in turn makes the development of new surgical techniques much easier.

Tools of the trade

Many of the surgical instruments used 50 years ago are still in use today. Scalpels, scissors, forceps and clamps are still used because surgeons need instruments to cut into the body, to prevent bleeding and to join bits together again! However, things are beginning to change in a radical way – in another fifty years, surgical instruments may no longer be recognizable!

For a surgeon, cutting into a living person is a fundamental part of the job. But the cutting edge of surgery is no longer a simple scalpel – in future you could be opened up using anything from water to microwaves!

Looking the part

Operating teams are always recognizable in their sterile gowns and gloves. But the gloves they wear have recently undergone a number of developments. Some doctors and patients are allergic to the latex that was used to make surgical gloves – in fact at least one patient is thought to have died as a result. So new **polymers** are now used which make the gloves safer for doctors and patients alike. An even more serious problem has been the risk to health workers of operating on patients with problems like **hepatitis**, **HIV** or **AIDS**. A small cut on the skin of a doctor or nurse during surgery could leave the doctors and nurses open to infection by very serious or incurable diseases. Here again, polymer technology has come to the rescue. Gloves made of para-aramidic fibre, a tough new polymer, are virtually impossible to cut – they are five times more resistant to a blade than the equivalent weight of steel!

Taking us apart...

Diamonds, best known for their beautiful looks in jewellery, are the hardest naturally-occurring material and have long been used for cutting in industry. In the last 25 years, the medical profession has increasingly turned to diamond-edged scalpels when particularly fine, clean cuts are needed. Eye surgery is probably the best example of this. The great majority of cataract operations are now carried out using diamond scalpels because of the clean, precise cuts they make. What is more, a scalpel is being developed which emits light so the surgeon can see what is happening and also, through its diamond-coated laser-emitting blade, cauterises the tissue and stops bleeding as it cuts!

Martin Evans, a researcher in Bath, UK, is working on a way of cutting away areas of tissue using microwaves – the same sort of electromagnetic waves used to heat food in a microwave oven can be used to burn away tissue in a controlled way. He has tried the technique on areas of the **cervix** that needed to be removed and found it very effective and controllable. Another area where microwave cutting is being investigated is in the control of **atrial fibrillation**, where the two upper chambers of the heart beat very rapidly and ineffectively.

... with water?

What about cutting with water? In the UK, Mr Sami Shimi at the University of Dundee and Julian Minns and Dr Gregory-Smith at Durham are just some of the researchers who are currently investigating the possibility of using incredibly fine, high-pressure jets of water to cut away **tumours** inside the body with minimal damage to the surrounding blood vessels and other tissues. Using water, the whole process is cool so it doesn't heat the surrounding tissues. This helps to keep damage to a minimum.

23

Putting us back together

Taking people apart is one thing. Putting them back together successfully is quite another. After surgery, both the main opening and the many tiny internal blood vessels that are damaged can bleed quite a bit. This can be a serious problem, particularly after transplants and other major surgery. The more effectively the wound can be closed up, the better and faster the healing process will be.

For many years stitches (**sutures**) were the only way to do this, and an unpleasant experience for patients a week or two after surgery was the ritual of 'taking the stitches out.' These old-fashioned nylon stitches are still used – they are cheap, easy to use and provide an opportunity for medical staff to check up on the progress of their patient. However, in recent years things have moved on fast. One of the first big advances was the development of 'dissolving' stitches, which break down by themselves and fall out without needing a doctor or nurse to remove them.

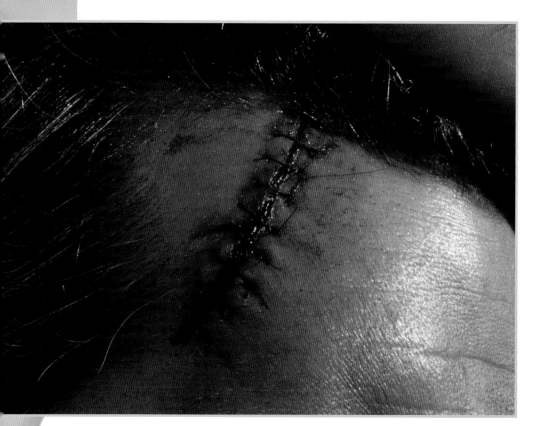

Using adhesives to replace stitching can be a big advantage, leading to a faster recovery, less pain and less scarring for the patient.

Surgical glue

But stitches are no longer the only option. Tiny clamps, staples, tape and even special glues are being used to close up surgical sites. Clamps and staples still need to be removed, but the most exciting development is the **adhesives**. Medical staff in casualty departments noticed that ordinary household glues could stick skin together very effectively, because of the numbers of people with fingers stuck together that they had to deal with!

Once the potential for using glues instead of stitches had been recognized, a variety of different surgical adhesives were developed, and more are currently being researched. Using glue rather than stitches makes the surgery much shorter, and considerably reduces the risk of bleeding. Surgical adhesives are one of the innovations that have made multiple organ transplants possible over the last ten years.

ADAL-2

In Spain, research into new adhesives for eye surgery is well under way. One of them, ADAL-2, has been tried in human eye operations. The glue is elastic, so no strain is put on the eye tissues, and it is biodegradable, so that as the tissues heal, it disappears. In the results of a trial of 50 patients who had eye surgery, some had conventional stitches and some had the new adhesive. Medically, the performance was similar, but the patients much preferred the adhesive. Here, the doctor in charge of the trial summarizes the findings:

'We didn't find any difference regarding inflammation or residual material, but patients expressed less discomfort when the adhesive was used. We should consider these products as a valid alternative to sutures with comparable efficacy and higher patient satisfaction.'
M. Emilia Mulet Homs MD, PhD

25

Life support systems

People cannot live without a constant supply of food and oxygen to the cells in their bodies. A build-up of poisonous waste can be fatal too. Yet when major organs like the heart and lungs have to be removed in transplant surgery, the body can be without a beating heart for several hours and when surgery is carried out to repair damage in the heart itself, the beating must be stilled to allow the delicate operation to take place. Until the 1950s, heart surgery was very limited. The patient was cooled down to slow the speed of their body reactions and even then, the surgery on the heart could only last a few minutes before tissue damage set in.

Heart-lung machines

In 1953, Dr John Gibbon developed the first **heart-lung machine** and thanks to this amazing piece of technology, surgery on the heart that lasts several hours can now be carried out as a matter of routine. The machine works by taking over the job of the heart and lungs. It pumps blood out of the body, puts oxygen into the blood and removes the carbon dioxide. The blood is then returned to the body.

The machine monitors the temperature of the blood and the oxygen and carbon dioxide levels of the patient all the time. Various other things shown by the machine are all monitored individually to keep the patient safe.

Complete body support

The basic heart-lung machine has moved on so that doctors now have access to complete life support systems. Severely injured or ill patients have to be connected up to a life support system simply to stabilize their condition and keep them alive before surgery can take place. Similarly, after surgery, some patients will be on life support for a considerable amount of time. Even if someone is effectively dead, with no brain activity at all, they can be kept apparently alive on a life support machine.

What are the ethics?

This technology raises ethical dilemmas for doctors and families alike. How long should someone be kept 'alive' in the hope that the medicine of the future might help them? Science cannot answer questions like these – the solutions need to be found by the family of the patient and their doctors, and by society as a whole (which has to fund the machines).

How the heart-lung machine works

The heart-lung machine can be used to stabilize patients before surgery, keep them alive during surgery and help them to recover after surgery. The machine is connected directly into the heart of the patient. The flow of blood in the machine is managed by a member of the surgical team known as the perfusionist, who keeps a close eye on all the monitors of the heart-lung machine and makes adjustments to ensure that the patient's blood is kept as stable as possible. At the end of the surgery, the perfusionist will make sure that the patient's own circulation takes over very gradually and gently from the machine.

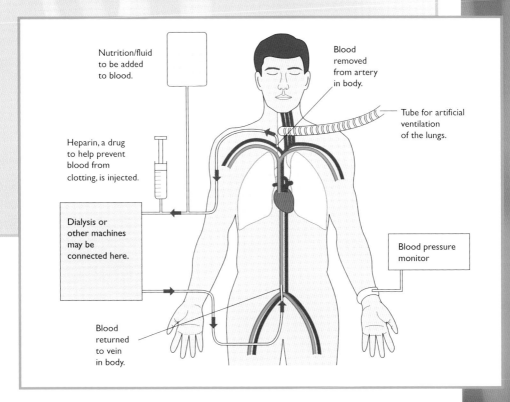

Nutrition/fluid to be added to blood.

Blood removed from artery in body.

Tube for artificial ventilation of the lungs.

Heparin, a drug to help prevent blood from clotting, is injected.

Dialysis or other machines may be connected here.

Blood pressure monitor

Blood returned to vein in body.

The Octopus™ – a new generation

Heart surgery has become common. As people live longer, they are more likely to suffer from heart diseases of various kinds. Lifestyles that include lots of fatty foods and smoking but very little exercise also increase the risk of heart disease. Each year, around 750,000 patients worldwide undergo a particular type of heart surgery called a coronary bypass, in which damaged and diseased blood vessels that supply blood to the heart itself are removed and replaced. The vast majority of these patients undergo this surgery with their hearts stopped and their blood flowing through a heart-lung machine. But an exciting new discovery that was first used in 1997 means that some of these operations can take place without stopping the heart.

The Octopus™ is one example of a new type of surgical device known as a stabilizer. Surgeons can use stabilizers to stop just a small part of the heart from moving. In the case of the Octopus™ this is done using small vacuum cups that are fixed around the area of the heart where the surgery needs to be done. Stabilizers cannot replace heart-lung machines, but they can avoid total stoppage of the heart in some cases, making the whole procedure less traumatic for the patient and the surgeons alike.

'This procedure [using stabilizers] works best in patients with blockages of the arteries that are easy to reach.'
James Magovern, M.D,
Assistant professor of
Surgery, Allegheny
General Hospital, USA

The development of new technology like the Octopus™ is making heart surgery quicker and safer for patients and doctors alike.

Bloodless surgery

Surgery is often linked to blood loss, which always carries a risk to the patient. If a patient loses too much blood, they will be given a **transfusion** where blood from a donor is used to make up for what they have lost. However, there are some groups of people for whom blood transfusions raise real ethical dilemmas. Jehovah's Witnesses are a religious group with deeply held beliefs forbidding them to accept blood transfusions. 'Bloodless' surgery has been developed to overcome the problem of individuals dying because they refuse life-saving treatment that involves blood transfusions. There are a number of techniques that make bloodless surgery possible. Patients can be treated with drugs before surgery, so their bodies make extra blood. This enables them to withstand some blood loss more easily. The body is cooled to very low temperatures during surgery to slow the circulation as much as possible, and every cut is **cauterized** immediately to prevent bleeding.

Bloodless surgery is becoming more and more common, regardless of the beliefs of the patient. It reduces the general rate of post-operative infections and removes the risk of infection from blood products or any allergic reactions as a result of transfusions. Perhaps in the future, bloodless surgery will become the norm rather than the exception.

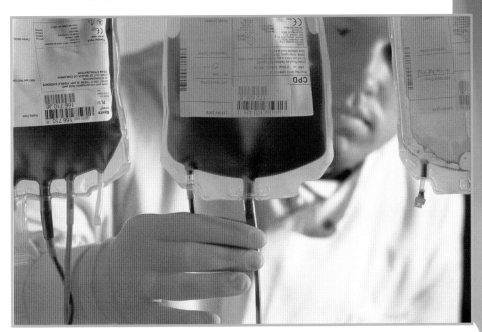

Blood transfusion services often struggle to persuade enough people to give blood to supply the needs of all the patients who need transfusions. Bloodless surgery may solve this problem in the future.

Keyhole surgery and microsurger

Surgery, even modern surgery, is not without its risks. Two of the biggest risks associated with making a cut into someone, operating inside them and then closing up wound are bleeding and infection. New techniques such as keyhole surgery and microsurgery are making a big contribution to reducing those risks. With a large wound, lots of small blood vessels are cut, increasing the chances of bleeding after the operation. At best, bleeding like this is a worry and needs blood transfusions and even more surgery to stop it. At worst, the blood loss is so great that the patient dies, as we saw in the case of the Bijani twins on page 17. What is more, a large wound gives microorganisms a much bigger area in which to get into

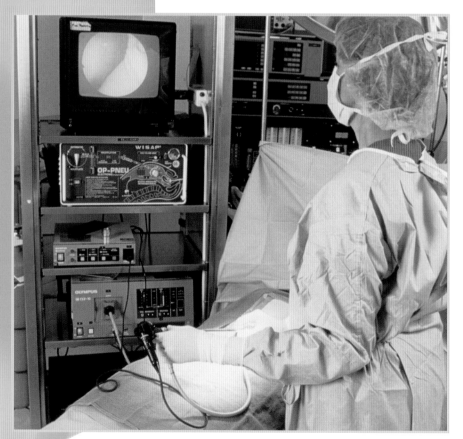

The development of keyhole surgery has involved not only the production of completely new and specialized surgical instruments, but also a completely different way for surgeons to operate. Carrying out a procedure whilst watching what you are doing on a screen takes a lot of skill, and training!

the body – and even the cleanest operating theatre will hold a few germs. Post-operative infections can be fatal as the infective organisms get straight into the blood stream, and are often **antibiotic-resistant**. However, there are two new techniques that are moving surgery forward in many different ways, including reducing the likelihood of both post-operative bleeding and infection.

Keyhole surgery

Keyhole surgery is the popular name for laparoscopic surgery. It involves making tiny holes instead of large ones in the body wall. In small children, these may be as small as three millimetres in diameter. Metal tubes are placed in the holes to hold them open while special surgical instruments, which have been developed just for keyhole surgery, are fed into the body. Carbon dioxide is pumped into the body cavity to inflate it and make more room for the surgeon to see what is going on. With such tiny incisions, how does the surgeon actually manage to see what is happening? One of the tubes (the laparoscope) carries **optical fibres** that provide light and a telescope, which is attached to a tiny video camera that projects video images onto a television screen in the operating theatre. The surgeon manipulates the instruments from the outside of the body, and controls what they are doing by watching what is happening on the television screen.

The advantages

Keyhole surgery was first used with adults and the advantages are many. They include:
- Smaller incisions so there is very little scarring – the cuts are so small they often don't even need stitching.
- Less pain after the operation.
- Less risk of infection from healing wounds.
- Quicker recovery time.
- Shorter hospital stays which makes keyhole surgery considerably cheaper.

Keyhole surgery has revolutionized many everyday procedures, such as the removal of gall bladders when they are full of **gall stones**. This operation used to involve a large cut along the abdomen and a stay in hospital that lasted from several days to over a week. Now most patients have keyhole surgery and are in hospital only overnight. Other routine operations like **hernia** repairs have similarly been hugely improved through keyhole techniques – in fact many hernia patients don't even have to stay in hospital overnight any more.

Children and keyholes

In 1990, Mr Hock Tan, a **paediatric** surgeon working in Australia, realized that although he would like to try keyhole surgery for children, the specialized surgical instruments would be too big for their tiny bodies. He persuaded some surgical instrument makers to develop a range of keyhole instruments specifically designed to be used on small children.

Once Professor Tan had the instruments he needed, he set about developing keyhole techniques that were suitable for the problems that affect small children. His success has resulted in doctors from around the world joining him to learn about this very delicate surgery. Keyhole surgery on children is immensely skilled work, but it is worth it for all the benefits it brings. The techniques are still very new, so this is an area that is sure to expand enormously in years to come.

'The only instruments available … were often bigger than the babies!'

Professor Hock Tan

Professor Hock Tan – his inspirational work on keyhole surgery in children has opened up a whole new area of the most delicate surgical technique.

Mason's story

When Professor Hock Tan was working at Great Ormond Street Children's Hospital, London, he met Carol Sweeney and her little son, Mason. As a newborn baby Mason thrived, but within a couple of weeks he stopped gaining weight. This wasn't surprising, because every time he fed, he vomited his milk back violently. He had **pyloric stenosis**, a thickening of the muscle at the base of the stomach that prevents food passing through into the rest of the gut. The condition ran in Carol's family. Her father had the condition and had major surgery when he was a baby which left him with a large scar. Carol herself also had a scar across her abdomen from the surgery she had when she was two months old. She had to stay in hospital for two weeks after surgery to recover.

When doctors confirmed that Mason had pyloric stenosis, he received very different treatment. The operation to split open the pyloric muscle, so that food could pass into his gut, was done by Professor Tan, using keyhole surgery. Mason was only in hospital for a couple of days, and has virtually no scars – just two tiny puncture marks on his tummy and a small cut by his tummy button, scars which will fade to virtually nothing by the time he grows up. He recovered quickly from the surgery and is now feeding normally and growing well.

The difference in the three generations of Mason's family shows clearly just how far surgery has come, and laparoscopic techniques are going to keep on developing. More and more different types of surgery will come to be done with the help of a laparoscope, some very tiny instruments and a very skilled surgeon. Operations on babies like Mason and even operating on a baby before it is born are all possible now – who knows what will be possible in the future? Keyhole surgery is one of the new techniques that will probably become the norm in years to come, making conventional surgery seem primitive in comparison.

Microsurgery

The development of keyhole surgery has brought about a change in technique in many operations. Surgeons now only need to make tiny holes just millimetres across in a body in order to perform surgery. Microsurgery involves surgeons operating whilst looking through glasses with magnifying lenses (loupes) or through a microscope, and carrying out surgical procedures magnified in this way. Surgeons can now repair arteries, veins, damaged nerves and injuries to muscles in a way that was simply not possible a few years ago.

Why is microsurgery needed?

Most of our blood vessels and nerves are very small, but there are many occasions when a surgeon really needs to be able to perform surgery on these tiny body parts – for example, to rejoin a severed finger or to reconstruct a damaged face and give back facial expressions. This is when microsurgery comes into its own.

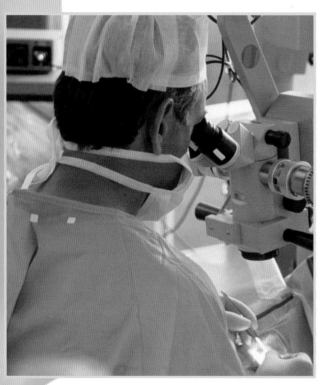

Loupes magnify what a surgeon sees by 3.5 to 4.5 times. A microscope gives even greater magnification, and can be linked to video monitors to allow surgeons to teach as they operate.

Only the microsurgeon can see what he or she is doing. He or she wears a headpiece that acts as a binocular microscope, and uses specially manufactured instruments that are exceptionally small. The thread used to stitch up the patient is so fine that it is virtually invisible to the naked eye. It takes an enormous amount of skill to work under magnification, where every tiny movement of your hand appears huge and the smallest tremor can undo much careful work. But more and more surgeons are taking the time to learn these new and complex skills, because of the benefits they bring to patients.

The benefits of microsurgery

One of the main benefits of microsurgery is in reattaching severed limbs and other body parts. The blood vessels and major nerves of the severed part can be reattached to the rest of the body so that in many cases, the injured person gets back, for example, a hand or foot that still works, although the fine movements are sometimes lost.

Sometimes, as a result of disease or accidents, people lose the ability to control their facial muscles and lose their expressions. So much of our communication depends on our facial expressions that this can leave them feeling isolated and unable to communicate. Microsurgery allows surgeons to attach new muscles and nerves into the face to give it back a range of expressions, improving the quality of life for the patient immensely. In 2003, a team of surgeons in Austria successfully transplanted a tongue from a dead donor into a man whose tongue had been removed due to cancer. The join is so precise than the man should be able to eat and talk with his new organ, although no one is yet sure if he will be able to taste with it!

Microsurgery is improving the options available in the treatment of many different conditions. It has revolutionized the repair of lost digits, and had a massive impact on cosmetic surgery, where people choose to undergo surgery to improve their looks. It is also of vital importance in the new area of operating on babies before they are born.

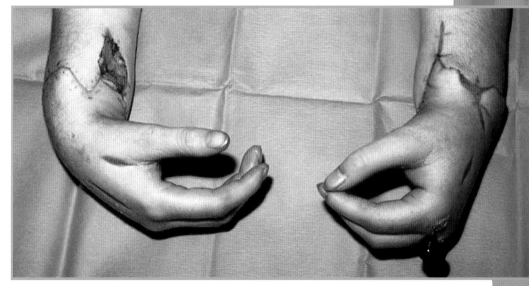

The ability of surgeons to reconnect tiny blood vessels and nerves as well as muscles and other tissues means that astonishing surgery, like reattaching severed limbs, has become possible.

Light and sound in surgery

The use of light in the form of lasers is a fast growing area of surgery. Lasers are very precise, so they don't damage the surrounding tissues. They work quickly, so they can speed up surgery and sterilize the surgical area, giving less risk of infection. They can be used in keyhole surgery, they cause less bleeding and swelling than in normal surgery and they make it possible to carry out more operations on a one-day basis. No wonder surgeons are constantly finding new ways to use them!

How laser works

Laser light is a beam of very focused, 'concentrated' light. Laser stands for **L**ight **A**mplification by **S**timulated **E**mission of **R**adiation. Electricity is used to excite the electrons in the solid, liquid or gas which is being used as the laser material to produce beam of light of very regular light waves, all moving in the same direction.

The light energy in a laser is all focused on a very tiny area, so it is very hot and very precise, which in turn makes it ideal for cutting and sealing wounds.

In eye surgery, lasers are increasingly used instead of conventional scalpels to remove very thin layers of tissue from the surface of the eye to correct sight problems such as **short sightedness**, **long sightedness** and **astigmatism**.

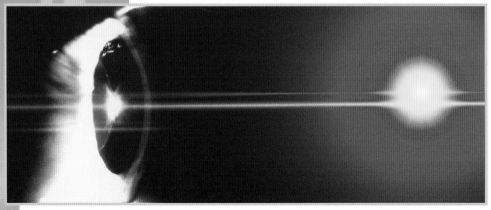

For many people, removing a tiny amount of tissue enables their eyes to focus clearly again. A laser's precise beam makes it very effective for delicate eye surgery.

The surgeon delivers pulses of laser light, and each pulse removes around 0.001 mm (or 39 millionths of one inch) of tissue in milliseconds! The whole procedure is very fast and precise – an advantage for both the patient and the surgeon.

Lasers are also being used more and more in both plastic surgery and cosmetic surgery, to remove growths in the skin as well as unwanted tattoos and scars. They produce very little bleeding because they seal the blood vessels as they remove the tissue – this also reduces the risk of infection. Lasers are used to seal blood vessels to prevent bleeding during some conventional surgery, and they are also used to activate some of the new medical **adhesives** (see page 24–5).

Lasers and cancer

One of the most feared diseases in the developed world is cancer, because even with all our sophisticated medicine, it is still difficult to treat and cure. Lasers are one of the new weapons in the fight against cancer. They can be used to remove tumours, and to destroy the cancerous tissue. They are also used simply to shrink some tumours that cannot be otherwise treated, by vapourizing some of the tissue. This can make the patient more comfortable if nothing else.

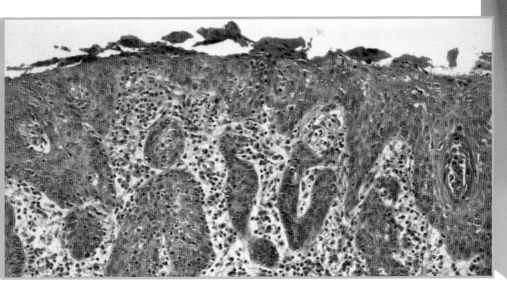

Some cancers, like this **tumour** on the vocal cords, are particularly suited to treatment with lasers. In future, cancer treatment may come to rely on these amazing light systems more and more.

Photodynamic therapy

There are two new ways in which lasers are now used to treat cancers. One is to use heat from lasers to cut off the blood supply to tumours and so stop them growing. The other is **photodynamic therapy**. Patients are given chemicals that become poisonous to cells when they are exposed to laser light. The active tumour 'soaks up' the chemicals and then lasers are focused directly on the tumour. This starts up a chemical reaction, producing a toxin that in turn destroys the tumour. The surrounding tissue isn't affected because it isn't exposed to the laser light and there are few side effects. This treatment offers real hope for cancer sufferers in the future.

Ultrasound and surgery

The use of **ultrasound** scanners in detecting and identifying problems for the surgeon before surgery begins has already been discussed (see page 14). But the technology is also being increasingly used during surgery to monitor a number of things. For example, one team have used ultrasound scanning during surgery on patients with a form of cancer that causes growths to develop on their kidneys. Once the surgeons have removed all the visible growths, they use ultrasound to scan the kidneys. They have found that they could identify additional tumours in 25 per cent of their patients. By using ultrasound during surgery, they can make sure that as many tumours as possible are removed, reducing the likelihood of having to operate again.

Ultrasound in emergency

When soldiers are injured on the battlefield, or ambulance crews race to a disaster, the doctors and surgeons have to act as fast as possible to save lives. The use of high-intensity focused ultrasound (HIFU) is another new area that is being considered particularly important for surgeons. A unit is being developed which will use low-intensity ultrasound to see inside injured people and find out where any internal bleeding is taking place. A focused beam of high-intensity ultrasound can then be delivered to exactly the right spot to actually seal the blood vessels and stop the bleeding. This will gain precious time in which to get the casualty to a fully-equipped hospital. Both soldiers and civilians stand to gain from the development of technologies like these.

Similarly, ultrasound is being used during brain surgery, to make sure that all traces of tumours are removed, and in surgery on the vessels of the heart to help check that all blockages have been removed. A new technique using ultrasound to monitor the levels of body fluids in patients is also helping to make sure that people recover more rapidly from surgery and are less likely to need a fluid drip or blood transfusion after surgery. Patients who are monitored by ultrasound during major surgery leave hospital on average two days earlier than patients who are not monitored in this way.

Lithotripsy – sound in action

Kidney and bladder stones are caused by a build up of chemicals in these body parts. They can be excruciatingly painful, and used to need surgery to remove them. Now in many cases, ultrasound can also be used to treat patients much more easily. In the process known as lithotripsy, ultrasound or ordinary sound is used to generate shock waves that travel through the body to a precise focus point and shatter kidney and bladder stones. This development, which has come about in the last 20 years, has had a massive impact in reducing the amount of surgery that takes place.

The whole process of lithotripsy can be carried out with the patient fully conscious. Once the kidney stones have been broken up, they are simply passed out in the urine as tiny sand-like particles.

Pioneering foetal surgery

Keyhole surgery, microsurgery, ultrasound techniques and lasers all have a part to play in one of the most controversial new areas of surgical expertise – that of foetal surgery (operating on a developing baby before birth). Detailed blood tests and ultrasound scanning have made it increasingly possible for doctors to diagnose problems in a baby long before it is born. Often this information is used to make decisions about whether the pregnancy should continue, or to plan for surgery immediately after birth. But increasingly, there are situations where the surgeons can intervene while the baby is still in its mother's womb. Some of the techniques described here are widely used and few people question them any more, but others are very new indeed and some people are concerned about the ethics of what is being done.

Changing the blood

For most developing babies, the safest place they can possibly be is in their mother's body. But for a small number of pregnancies, the womb

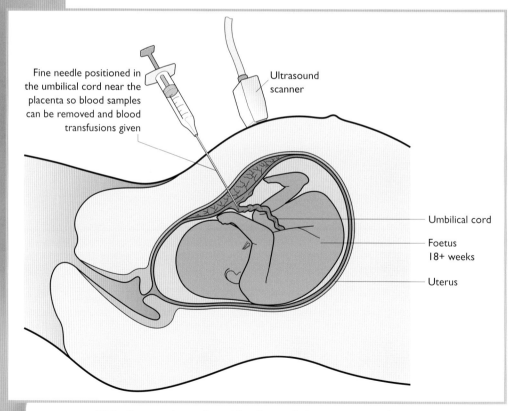

Fine needle positioned in the umbilical cord near the placenta so blood samples can be removed and blood transfusions given

Ultrasound scanner

Umbilical cord

Foetus 18+ weeks

Uterus

This diagram shows how blood transfusions are carried out before birth. Some babies need more than one transfusion if they are to survive until the end of the pregnancy.

becomes a death trap when the mother's body sets out to destroy the baby growing within her. The problems usually arise because of incompatibility between the blood groups of the mother and the baby. The mother makes **antibodies** against her baby's blood, and as a result the developing child suffers from severe **anaemia** and can die.

In the past, babies affected like this had a high chance of dying before or soon after birth. Now, thanks to surgery that takes place before they are born, most of them live. Ultrasound imaging allows doctors to see what is happening as they carry out blood **transfusions** into the umbilical cord itself. A tube is passed through the body wall of the mother, through the wall of the uterus and into the vein in the umbilical cord to allow the transfusion to take place. This surgery can start at 18 weeks of pregnancy (a normal pregnancy lasts for 40 weeks).

Pioneering work

It is now possible to carry out some quite drastic surgery on unborn babies. In Florida, USA, Dr Ruben Quintero has developed a revolutionary keyhole surgical technique to save the lives of identical twins suffering from twin-to-twin transfusion (TTTS) problems, where a problem in the blood vessels of the shared placenta results in one twin getting more blood and **amniotic fluid** than the other. One twin becomes large and swollen, the other small and shrunken, and in 90% of severe cases both twins die.

Identical twins can be at special risk during pregnancy because they share a placenta. With his revolutionary new laser surgery, Dr Quintero offers hope – if other doctors follow his lead.

Laser surgery in the womb

Dr Quintero identifies the faulty blood vessels and then, using keyhole instruments, makes an incision in the mother's abdomen and womb and uses a laser to seal off the faulty vessels. The fluid levels should then return to normal. After more than 100 of these amazing operations, Dr Quintero has an 84% survival rate for one twin, and a 40–50% survival rate for both. Because of his successes, more doctors are beginning to undertake this very delicate but life-saving procedure.

More trailblazing

Another American surgeon, Dr Joe Bruner, has developed a completely different form of surgery on unborn babies. One groundbreaking aspect of his work is with foetuses that have **spina bifida**. When a baby develops normally, the spinal cord is protected by the **vertebrae**. In spina bifida, part of this bony protection is missing and so the spinal cord is exposed. The spinal nerves can easily be damaged, and this in turn can lead to the child being paralysed. Normally doctors operate as soon as possible after a baby is born, and cover the exposed spinal cord with a protective plate, but often damage has already been done in the womb and during birth.

Joe Bruner believes that if the surgery can be carried out before birth, the risk of severe long-term disability can be reduced. He carries out an amazing procedure at around 23 weeks of pregnancy. First he cuts into the woman's abdomen and moves her womb out of her body, but without detaching it completely. He then opens up the womb itself to expose the foetus with its malformed spine. The team then try to create a layer of tissue to protect the tiny spinal cord as much as they can before returning it to the womb and stitching everything back together again. This surgery is very risky, because it could easily trigger contractions that would lead to the baby being born prematurely and perhaps not surviving.

Dr Bruner is convinced that his cutting-edge surgery has the potential to reduce the disability associated with spina bifida, but not all doctors are convinced. The results have not produced clear evidence either way. So far, the children born after Joe Bruner's surgery have certainly not been disability free, but who can say what they would have been like without this procedure?

But is it ethical?

When new surgical techniques emerge, people will question whether it is ethical to try out treatments on patients who are already ill. Often patients give their consent and are happy to take part in trials of new treatments in the hope that, even if they don't benefit personally, someone else will in the future. But when the new treatment is being carried out on an unborn child, who has no way of giving consent, there are some big ethical issues to consider. The parents are, naturally, deeply distressed to find that their unborn child has problems – can they really give impartial and informed consent for new surgery to be tried? How much do they understand of the risks, both of the surgery itself and the possibility of triggering labour?

Many doctors feel that the benefits seen so far as a result of these new surgical techniques do not justify the risks taken, and that perhaps foetal surgery is a step too far. Yet the prospect of healing before birth, when it is possible to allow a fit and healthy child to be born, will surely keep surgeons trying until they are successful.

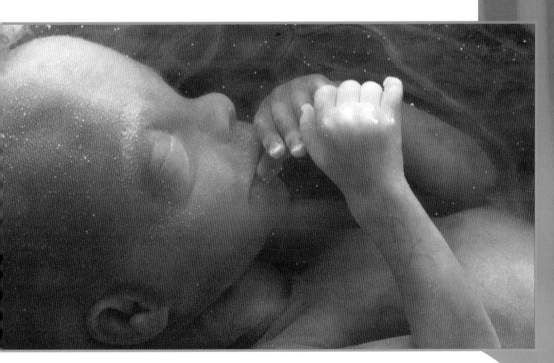

Not just 'Can it be done?' but also 'Should it be done?' Would a developing foetus choose surgery that might offer it the chance of normal life – or reject surgery to make sure of a safe delivery into the world? We don't know the answer. This is one reason why foetal surgery is still so controversial.

Robot surgeons

The idea of a robot surgeon sounds like something from *Star Wars*. But robot surgeons are no longer science fiction – in the last few years they have become science fact! Robot-assisted surgery is becoming accepted in more and more areas of medicine, and it has a number of real advantages. Robots can carry out procedures on a much smaller scale than their human counterparts – the stitches of a robot surgeon are unbelievably tiny and neat – and they do not suffer from shaking hands!

Remote control

One area where robots have been found to be very useful in assisting human surgeons is in heart-bypass surgery. In the traditional way of carrying out heart bypass surgery, the chest is opened up and the heart stopped while the patient is put on a **heart-lung machine**. Using robot surgeons and the latest techniques, the surgery can be carried out as keyhole surgery through three tiny incisions. One 'arm' of the robot is the endoscope carrying light and a camera into the body. Other arms hold the surgical instruments and the surgeon controls the movements of the robot from a computer console, using foot pedals to control the camera and zoom in and out. Robotic surgery is still so new that doctors are in the process of assessing just how much benefit it brings to

Heart disease

The heart is a bag of muscle which pumps blood around your body, about 70 times a minute from before you are born to the day you die, supplying food and oxygen to the cells of the body. To beat properly, the heart muscle needs a good blood supply and this is supplied by the coronary arteries. Sometimes, the walls of the coronary arteries become clogged up with fatty deposits. If the blood supply to the heart muscle is cut off, a heart attack and possible death results. So if a patient develops symptoms due to blocked coronary arteries, surgeons will carry out heart bypass surgery, where they reroute the blood supply to the heart using blood vessels taken from other places in the body, such as the legs.

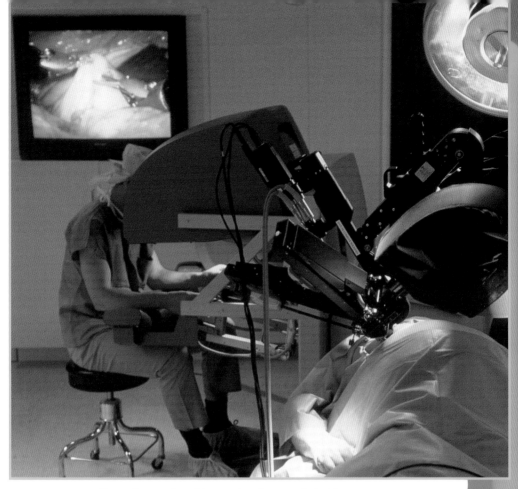

Every human hand has a tiny degree of shakiness – even surgeons. Robot surgeons never shake! Robot assistants may be present in every operating theatre in the future.

patients. Some people question whether the money spent developing robot systems (which, so far, mainly mimic the work of human surgeons) is justified. Others argue that as they become more refined and more widely used they will become more cost-effective and capable of doing more things. What is more, they may raise the quality of care available in developing countries – but only if the technology is affordable.

Development of robotic operating systems is an exciting new technological challenge that is being taken up in many different places. For example, engineers at NASA are developing a robotic arm called RAMS which will be able to make smooth precise motions as small as 25 millionths of a meter, the width of a human hair. The hope is that it will make surgery on delicate areas like the eye, the ear and the brain much more effective and safe.

Surgery at a distance

In September 2001, a groundbreaking operation took place. A woman in Strasbourg, Austria, had her gall bladder removed using keyhole surgery. Nothing unusual about that – except that the surgeons who carried out the operation were almost 4000 miles away in the USA! The actual operation was carried out by a robotic surgeon in France, controlled by instructions relayed through a computer system from Michel Gagner, chief of the Department of Laparoscopic Surgery at Mount Sinai Medical Center in New York, and Jacques Marescaux of the University of Strasbourg. The operation itself was straightforward, and the patient, who had given her consent to being part of the experiment, made a rapid recovery. The reason the technique generated so much excitement was because of its potential uses in the future. Surgeons with specialist expertise in rare conditions will be able to operate on patients anywhere in the world, at the same time passing on their expertise to colleagues. It opens the door for people in the developing world to have access to the standards of health care already commonplace in countries like the UK, the USA and Australia. The only problem is the cost – at the moment, because it is so new, robot surgery is extremely expensive and so only available in the developed world.

The man behind the machines

The idea for using robots in surgery owes much to the work of Brian Davies, who has been made the first ever Professor of Medical Robotics at Imperial College, London, after pioneering a whole range of medical robots. The first work Professor Davies carried out in the medical field was designing systems to help people born without limbs as a result of the **thalidomide** tragedy in the 1970s. From that point onwards he realized the potential for robotics in medicine and he has pushed the boundaries of what is possible ever since.

In 1991, working with Dr Roger Hibberd, he was responsible for the first robot ever to remove tissue from a patient. Since then he has been involved in the design of a whole range of medical robots including the Acrobot, which is used in knee surgery, as well as machines to work on the nervous system and many other areas of surgery.

Professor Davies is not a surgeon himself, although he spends a great deal of time working with surgeons and watching operations to find out what is needed and where a robot system can be most helpful. His pioneering work is sure to have a massive impact on the success of different types of surgery for many years to come.

'Our hopes for the future are to make smaller, simpler, robots that can be used for delicate tasks such as spine surgery, in which part of the vertebra is machined away without damaging the spinal cord. There is still much research to be done, but we feel our robots can provide real benefits to patients.'

Professor Brian Davies, speaking about the future of robotic surgery

Professor Brian Davies with his knee surgery robot. Not content with the pioneering work he has completed, Professor Davies has a vision for the future in which ever smaller robots help surgeons to carry out operations which at present simply cannot be done.

New parts for old

Some problems never go away. Human remains that are centuries old show signs of the wear and tear that indicates they suffered from painful **arthritis** when they were alive. Modern surgeons are still working on new ways to deal with the problems of arthritic joints – an increasingly important issue to deal with as the population gets older. For many years now one of the most common operations performed by an **orthopaedic** surgeon has been a hip replacement.

Artificial joints

The ball and socket joint at the hip, between the pelvis and the **femur**, takes a tremendous hammering during our active lives. The bones are covered with smooth rubbery cartilage and lubricated by a substance called synovial fluid. Arthritis often attacks the joint, destroying the cartilage and leaving the once smooth bone surfaces rough, with the bones grinding painfully over each other every time the joint moves.

The traditional replacement joint has been a plastic socket or cup fixed into the pelvis, with a metal head replacing

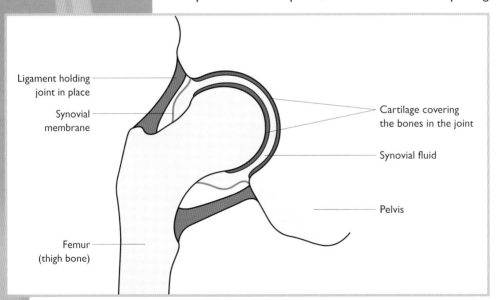

Ligament holding joint in place

Synovial membrane

Cartilage covering the bones in the joint

Synovial fluid

Pelvis

Femur (thigh bone)

The ball and socket joint, lubricated by synovial fluid, gives us a very wide range of movements forwards, backwards, sideways, up and down – try it!

the damaged bone of the femur. These joints have been very effective in many ways – they have given thousands of people a new lease of life free from pain. The biggest problem is that they can wear out and become loose. As the metal head moves in the socket, microscopic pieces of plastic and metal are shed. These pieces are about the same size as bacteria, and unfortunately they seem to trigger the body defences. They end up destroying the bone around the artificial joint, making it loose. More surgery is then needed to put things right, and this can often be more complicated than the original surgery to replace the joint.

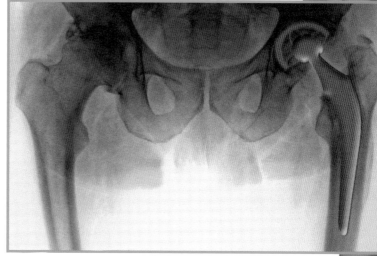

Artificial hip joints like this can give someone a new lease of life – now the challenge is to make sure the new joint lasts!

The hope is that new developments in synthetic materials will lead to artificial joints that have 20 to 30 years of active life in them. However, long-term studies will be needed to look at the way they behave when they are implanted in the body. What performs well in theory doesn't always live up to expectations in practice. Ceramic joints were thought to be the answer but problems with cracking means that there is still a long way to go before the perfect artificial joint is here.

A part for a heart

Normally, the valves of the heart stop the blood flowing backwards, so if things go wrong and the valves don't work it can be life-threatening. Fortunately they can be replaced by either an artificial valve made of plastic, a valve taken from an animal or a valve from a human donor, but there can be problems. The blood tends to clot around the artificial valve, so special coatings are being developed which reduce the problem. Growing new tissues from stem cells may help with the shortage of human valves in the future, while research into new artificial materials also continues.

Designer organs?

Producing replacement body parts from plastic and metal is one thing. Growing new human organs is quite another. Recent work on human stem cells, which have the potential to form different types of adult cells in the body, has made this prospect a real possibility. A team at the Bernard O' Brien Institute of Microsurgery in Australia have set out to 'tailor make' new organs from a patient's own body tissues. This would mean that no one need die waiting for an organ transplant, and it would also remove the need for the **immunosuppressant drugs**. Normally, when people are given a transplant, they have to take these drugs for the rest of their life to prevent their body rejecting the new organ. All drugs have some side effects and cost money, so an alternative to this lifetime of medication would be a big step forward.

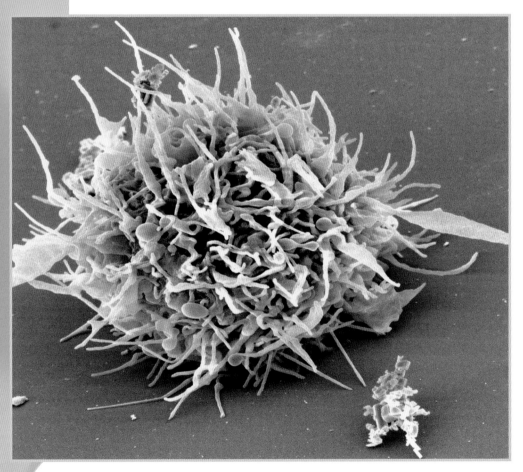

Using adult stem cells like these from a patient's own body, along with special scaffolding and a good blood supply, the team at the Bernard O'Brien Institute hope to be making designer organs within a few short years.

In an amazing new technique, surgeons at the Bernard O'Brien Institute create a space in the body of their patient and make a supporting structure in the chamber. Then, using microsurgery, they implant cells from the required organ, or stem cells, and a blood supply using the patient's own blood vessels. Once the circulation is in place, the new tissue will grow to the shape of the 'scaffolding'. It can then be removed and reattached, again using microsurgery, to the site where it is needed. In the near future, the team hope to be able to grow fat, muscle and bone tissue to repair and reconstruct parts of the body, and to be manufacturing new organs within their patient's own body!

Stem cell research

Scientists can grow tissue cells in the laboratory by providing them with specialized nutrients and the right conditions of oxygen, temperature and pH. For some years now they have been able to take skin cells from a patient and grow large sheets of new skin to replace tissue affected by burns. The technique was relatively limited until at the very end of 1998, two groups of American scientists announced a breakthrough. Both teams, one led by Dr James Thomson at Wisconsin and the other by John Gearhart in Baltimore, developed a technique for growing embryonic stem cells. Embryonic stem cells have the potential to become almost any of the specialized cells our body needs. This breakthrough raised hopes of a major medical advance – the ability to replace diseased or worn out body parts with new healthy tissue.

The new stem cell technology also raised many ethical issues, because the stem cells are derived from human embryos. Some people feel it is wrong to use spare embryos that have been produced for infertility treatment as a source of stem cells, even when the parents have given permission. The other source of embryonic stem cells is from aborted foetuses. Again, there are people who feel that abortion is wrong, and therefore that it is completely unacceptable to use aborted tissue to produce life-saving treatments.

These ethical concerns in turn drove more research to find and use the stem cells still present in our adult bodies. Now it seems that adult stem cells may have an important role in replacing and restoring damaged tissue. Although there are still many technical and ethical issues to be sorted out, the new techniques may well revolutionize medicine in the future.

When surgery goes wrong

In the developed world, it is easy to turn to surgery to solve our health problems instead of looking for ways to avoid the problems in the first place. For example, if people ate more healthily, stopped smoking, drank in moderation, took more exercise and drove more carefully to avoid traffic accidents, the need for surgery would largely disappear. It would save billions of pounds, but it involves major lifestyle changes – and unfortunately many people prefer to take risks and rely on surgeons to sort out the problems that result. But it is important to remember that not only does surgery cost a great deal of money but, even in the best surgical units, things sometimes go wrong.

From small problems…

When 16-year-old William broke his little finger and was told he needed surgery to insert wires to hold the bones together, it seemed a relatively minor procedure. But the

Mistakes made during surgery carried out late at night by a team who were not hand specialists have caused permanent damage to William's hand. He can only hope it doesn't affect him in his chosen career – he wants to be a doctor!

wires interfered with the first joint of the finger, which had been unaffected by the original break, leaving it unable to bend. William had to go through further surgery, followed by physiotherapy, to partially restore the function of the finger.

'I was so disappointed when I saw my finger after the surgery – I knew immediately that it wasn't right. It looked awful and the joint didn't bend at all. It's still not perfect, but at least now it works again!'
William Fullick, after corrective surgery carried out
by a different surgeon

…to complete disaster

When surgery is a last resort, with a patient who is seriously ill, the patient may die and no one is to blame. But in a small number of cases, errors during surgery lead to patients dying who would have otherwise lived.

Surgical **anaesthetics** kill a tiny number of people each year. The causes range from allergies to the anaesthetic drugs and equipment failure to errors by the anaesthetist. This can happen in minor surgery as well as during major operations, but the risk is very small, with problems only in approximately five operations out of every million carried out.

For other people, errors during surgery cause death. Blood vessels may be damaged causing massive bleeding. Sometimes, even the wrong operation is carried out. In the UK in 2000, a 69-year-old man went into hospital to have his diseased right kidney removed. The surgical team, however, removed his healthy left kidney – leaving him with no functioning kidneys at all. The consultant in charge of the case didn't read the notes, and the surgeon who carried out the operation ignored a warning from a student doctor that he was taking out the wrong kidney. Once the mistake was discovered everything possible was done, but the patient died five weeks later.

Today, surgeons are being encouraged to share difficult experiences to help others avoid the same problems. Honesty with patients and their relatives, along with a willingness to admit to mistakes, are helping to improve the situation for doctors and patients alike. This is important, because although most people who undergo surgery are delighted with the results, for those families where things go wrong, the consequences can last a lifetime.

Into the future

Surgeons fifty years ago would never have dreamed of operating through a tiny hole only millimetres wide, or using robots as assistants instead of other doctors, but these changes in surgery are only the beginning. Innovations already in the pipeline mean that surgery is going to be radically different again by the middle of the 21st century – in fact, it may almost disappear!

The sound of scalpels

In America, an astonishing research project has developed a futuristic scalpel that uses sound waves to destroy cancerous tissue. **Ultrasound** is used to pinpoint the **tumour**, and then high-intensity sound waves, far above the limits of human hearing, are precisely focused into the body. The sound waves destroy the diseased tissue by heat, but because they are so focused, have no effect on the surrounding healthy cells. This surgery involves no cutting, no bleeding and no risk of infection. It is already being tested on human beings, and the early trials removing parts of tumours have produced excellent results. 'Acoustic' scalpels could well be one of the most important surgical tools of the future.

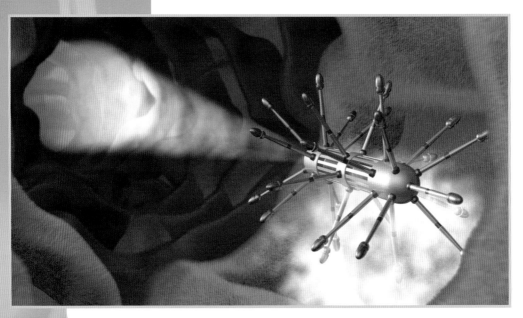

Nanomedicine is the stuff of science fiction, but with the development of nanobots like these, it is rapidly becoming science fact.

Nanomedicine – solutions in miniature

One of the most exciting predictions about the future of medicine is that much of the treatment will be at a **molecular** level. **Nanomedicine** is medicine on an almost unimaginably small scale. A nanometre (nm) is one billionth of a metre, or a millionth of a millimetre. **Nanotechnology** involves machines and techniques that work at this sub-microscopic level and nanobots are robots that can work on individual molecules. In future, nanobots may be able to operate on our DNA, mending our genes and curing genetic diseases. 'Cancer vaccines' of protective nanobots may mean that surgery takes place on individual cells as soon as they turn cancerous. Nanobots could carry new tissue cells to where they are needed to grow and repair damaged organs, replacing transplant surgery. Microscopic computer systems will be used to control armies of nanobot surgeons as they work in our bodies, solving problems without **anaesthetic** or the need to cut and stitch.

This kind of technology is still a long way off, but the development of the molecular structures needed to create nanobots is going well in laboratories around the world. Nanoparticle therapies are being tested in the treatment of breast cancer, brain **tumours** and as scaffolding for the growth of new bone in **orthopaedic** surgery.

Cyborgs – a reality?

Artificial limbs have come a long way since Victorian times, but a replacement hand that works under voluntary control is still a distant dream. Professor Kevin Warwick at Reading University had a silicon chip implanted into his arm which could communicate with computers around the university. In years to come it may be possible to use similar technology to control artificial limbs, which should become increasingly realistic both in appearance and, more importantly, in how they work.

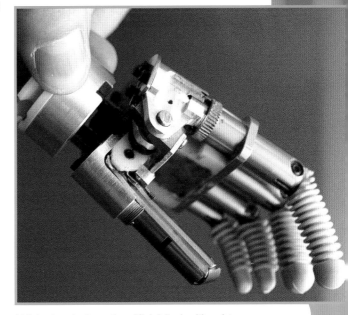

With the design of artificial limbs like this one, people who lose a limb will have brighter prospects for the future than at any other time in history.

Where should we draw the line?

With all of the advances that have taken place in surgery, some difficult ethical questions raise their heads. Just because certain surgical procedures are possible, does that mean they should actually be used, regardless of the drain on resources that may cause?

Another problem is that many of the newest technologies, from MRI scanners to the latest artificial limbs, are very expensive. This inevitably means that the most recent technology is not available to everyone. In some places the money will be there to buy whatever new equipment becomes available; in others the cash will not materialize, leading to great inequalities in the treatment of patients.

As surgical techniques continue to improve, another issue that needs to be considered is whether saving life is always the right thing to do. There are times when surgery can prevent death, but leave the patient with a poor quality of life. Some of the newest surgery on babies before and shortly after birth may save lives, but the babies can still suffer health problems. The decision about what is right to do, and when surgery should not be attempted, belongs to the patient, their family, the surgeon – and society as a whole.

'We don't want to, with surgery and other foetal therapy techniques, deliver babies who will survive, but with disastrous consequences. We have the moral right to decide not to do that.'
Dr Mark I Evans, Professor of Obstetrics and Gynaecology
and Director of the Center for Fetal Diagnosis and Therapy
at Wayne State University, Indiana, USA

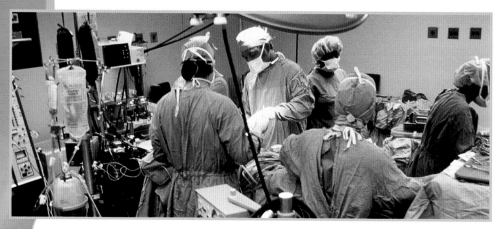

It is easy to think that all surgery is a good thing, but to safeguard its future, society needs to think carefully about what procedures should and should not be done.

It's your own fault...

There is another difficult question that needs to be addressed when resources are in short supply. A large proportion of the surgery that is carried out in our hospitals is for heart and lung disease, liver problems and to mend the damage caused in traffic accidents. How far should surgical resources – such as heart and lung surgery or organ transplants – be made available to people who are ill because they have abused their bodies with smoking, drinking, overeating or dangerous driving? Some people would argue that medical care should be available to everyone without any judgements being made about their behaviour. Other people feel it is a waste of resources to help people who have caused their own health problems and who are unlikely to change their behaviour even after treatment.

As a result of the tremendous dedication and expertise of the surgeons who use all the technology available to them, the quality of life for many thousands of patients is improved every day. However, society as a whole also needs to have an input into deciding which new technologies should be developed, how surgery should be used and where the ethical lines should be drawn. The possibilities for surgery are almost limitless – who knows what the future might hold?

The skills of the surgeon, coupled with some amazing new technology, help to give all of us the best chance of a long and healthy life.

Timeline

Stone Ages times (10,000 – 6000BC) Trepanning or simple brain surgery is carried out without **anaesthetics**.

Roman times The **Caesarean section** is apparently invented.

1163 The Pope decrees that monks and priests cannot be involved in surgery, opening the door to the barber-surgeons.

1745 The Company of Surgeons, which later became the Royal College of Surgeons, is formed.

1842 Dr Crawford Long uses **ether** as an anaesthetic for the first time, but does not publish his results until 1848.

1846 William Morton publishes his work on using ether as a dental anaesthetic.

1847 The use of **chloroform** as an anaesthetic in childbirth begins.

1851 Charles Chamberland improves the sterilizing of medical equipment and develops filters for bacteria that lead to the discovery of viruses.

1867 Joseph Lister starts to use phenol as an antiseptic in operating theatres, substantially reducing the death rate from infections.

1878 Measures such as keeping the operating theatre clean and washing hands before carrying out surgery make surgery even safer. This is known as **asepsis**.

1890 William Halsted, an American surgeon, introduces the practice of wearing rubber gloves during surgery.

1895 The German physicist Wilhelm Röntgen discovers **X-rays**.

1896 Three months after they were discovered, X-rays are used in medicine to help set broken bones. This is one of the fastest known transfers of a scientific discovery into a practical treatment.

1902 First successful kidney transplant is carried out on a dog.

1940s Surgery to replace hip joints using artificial joints is developed.

Heart pacemakers are developed.

1953 Dr John Gibson develops the first **heart-lung machine**.

1954 First successful human kidney transplant takes place in the USA between identical twin brothers.

1967 First successful human heart transplant is carried out.

1970s CT scanners developed.

Ultrasound scanning becomes increasingly sophisticated and widely used.

The anaesthetics halothane, enflurane and isoflurane are developed.

1977 The first full body MRI image is published.

1980s Whole body MRI scanners are used in hospitals.

1990 Professor Hock Tan starts to develop keyhole surgery for children.

1991 First use of a robot to remove human tissue during surgery.

1997 The Octopus™ stabiliser is used to stop only part of the heart during heart surgery.

1998 Embryonic **stem cells** are cultured in laboratories for the first time, opening the way for different types of cells and organs to be grown as needed for use in transplant surgery.

2000 Foetal surgery – operating on babies before birth – moves beyond blood **transfusions** to more complex procedures.

2001 Keyhole surgery is carried out on a woman in France by a robotic surgeon, controlled by doctors in the USA.

2003 The aepEX depth of anaesthesia monitor comes into use in hospitals.

A surgical team successfully transplants the tongue from a dead man to a living patient who had lost his tongue as a result of mouth cancer.

Glossary

adhesive glue

AIDS acquired immune deficiency syndrome. A fatal disease which affects the immune system, caused by HIV.

amniotic fluid the fluid which surrounds a foetus developing in the uterus (womb)

anaemia when the number of red blood cells (or the amount of haemoglobin) in the blood is too low to supply enough oxygen to the body tissues

anaesthesia loss of sensation to touch or pain, often linked to unconsciousness, produced by drugs before surgery

anaesthetic the chemical which causes the loss of sensation and consciousness before surgery

antibiotic-resistant microbe which is not destroyed by an antibiotic drug

antibodies special proteins made in the body in response to the presence of a foreign antigen

arthritis inflammation and stiffness of a joint

asepsis conditions free of all the microorganisms that can cause disease

astigmatism an eye condition where the curve of the cornea or lens of the eye is uneven, which gives 'fuzzy' vision

atom one of the tiny particles of which matter is made

atrial fibrillation condition where the upper chambers of the heart beat very fast and lose their rhythm

Caesarean section operation to deliver a baby through the wall of the mother's abdomen

cauterized when blood vessels are sealed using heat

cervix the lower part of the uterus that extends into the vagina

chloroform (trichloromethane) colourless, sweet smelling and poisonous chemical which was used as an early anaesthetic

compound substance made up of elements held together by chemical bonds to form a molecule

conjoined twins twins that are joined together at birth as a result of the early embryo failing to separate completely to form identical twins

ether (ethoxyethane) colourless, flammable liquid, which used to be used as an anaesthetic and is now mainly used as a solvent

femur the thigh bone

gall stones hard 'stones' which form in the gall bladder and bile duct and cause terrible pain

heart-lung machine machine which takes over the functions of the heart and lungs, supplying the blood with oxygen and pumping it around the body

hepatitis inflammation of the liver usually caused by infection by a virus

hernia where part of an internal organ bulges through a weak spot in the body wall

HIV human immunodeficiency virus

immunosuppressant drug drug that dampens down the action of the immune system – used after transplant surgery to prevent the body rejecting a new organ

long sightedness the ability to see distant objects more clearly than objects which are at close range, usually caused either by the shape of the eyeball or because the lens of the eye does not change shape effectively

magnetic field the area around a magnet where the magnetism can affect other objects

molecule two or more atoms joined together

nanomedicine/nanotechnology medicine and technology on an incredibly small scale, measured in nanometres

nitrous oxide also called laughing gas. A mild anaesthetic used in childbirth and after serious injuries.

optical fibre flexible fibre usually made of glass or plastic through which light can travel from one end to another to transmit images or data

orthopaedic the branch of medicine concerned with the treatment of problems of the bones, muscles and other tissues related to the skeleton

paediatric the branch of medicine concerned with the treatment of babies and small children

photodynamic therapy treatment where a medicine is activated by light

polymers large compound made up of repeating smaller units linked together

pyloric stenosis thickening of the muscle at the base of the stomach which prevents food passing through into the rest of the gut

radioisotope radioactive isotope of a chemical element

radio-opaque material through which X-rays cannot pass

short sightedness the ability to see close objects more clearly than objects which are at a distance, usually caused either by the shape of the eyeball or a misshapen cornea

spina bifida a condition where the vertebral column does not form properly as a foetus develops. The spinal cord bulges out and is often damaged by the time of birth.

stem cells 'immortal' cells that retain the ability to divide and multiply and to create other types of cell. Stem cells are found in embryos, bone marrow, skin, intestine and muscle tissue.

sutures stitches used in surgery

thalidomide a drug used to relieve the symptoms of morning sickness in pregnancy in the 1970s. It affected the development of the foetus and led to the birth of children with limbs that had not formed properly.

transfusion the transfer of blood from one person to another

tumour abnormal growth formed when cells grow in an uncontrolled way

ultrasound sound waves with a frequency of more than 20,000 hertz, too high for humans to hear

vertebrae the bones which make up the spine

X-ray high-energy electromagnetic radiation that can be used to make diagnostic images

Sources of information

Further reading

Science at the Edge: In Vitro Fertilization, Ann Fullick,
   (Heinemann Library, 2002)
Science at the Edge: Body Sculpting, Sally Morgan,
   (Heinemann Library, 2005)
Science at the Edge: Organ Transplantation, Ann Fullick,
   (Heinemann Library, 2002)

Websites

http://news.bbc.co.uk
A good source of many medical storylines – for example, medicine
through time and hope for spina bifida babies.
www.timelinescience.org
A website showing major scientific and medical discoveries over the
past thousand years.
www.thenakedscientists.com
Website covering many innovative medical techniques described by
different consultants. (Linked to an internet science radio programme
of the same name.)
http://www.fda.gov/fdac/features/1998/498_eye.html
Website exploring laser eye surgery.
www.mc.vanderbilt.edu/reporter/?ID=488
Web pages looking at ethical questions raised by advances in
foetal surgery.
http://cis.nci.nih.gov/fact/7_8.htm
Website produced by the National Cancer Institute looking at the
impact of lasers on cancer treatment.
http://cimu.apl.washington.edu/savingwithsound.html
Information about the use of ultrasound in medical treatment.

Author sources

The following materials were also used by the author in the writing
of this book:
Heinemann Advanced Science: Biology, Ann Fullick, (Heinemann, 2000)
Heinemann Advanced Science: Medical Physics Imaging, Jean Pope
(edited by Patrick Fullick), (Heinemann, 1999)
Institute of Physics Tutorial – Nanomedicine: Destination or Journey?

Index

Titles in the *Science at the Edge* series include:

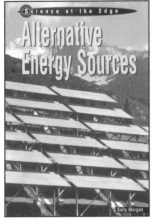

Hardback   0 431 14895 3

Hardback   0 431 14904 6

Hardback   0 431 14897 X

Hardback   0 431 14894 5

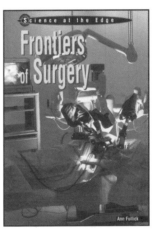

Hardback   0 431 14905 4

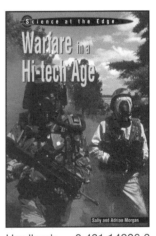

Hardback   0 431 14906 2

Hardback   0 431 14907 0

Hardback   0 431 14896 1

Find out about the other titles in the Heinemann Library on our website www.heinemann.co.uk/library